I Touched The Hem Of His Garment

Vini Tejas Pandya

PULON
PRESS
Burkhart Books

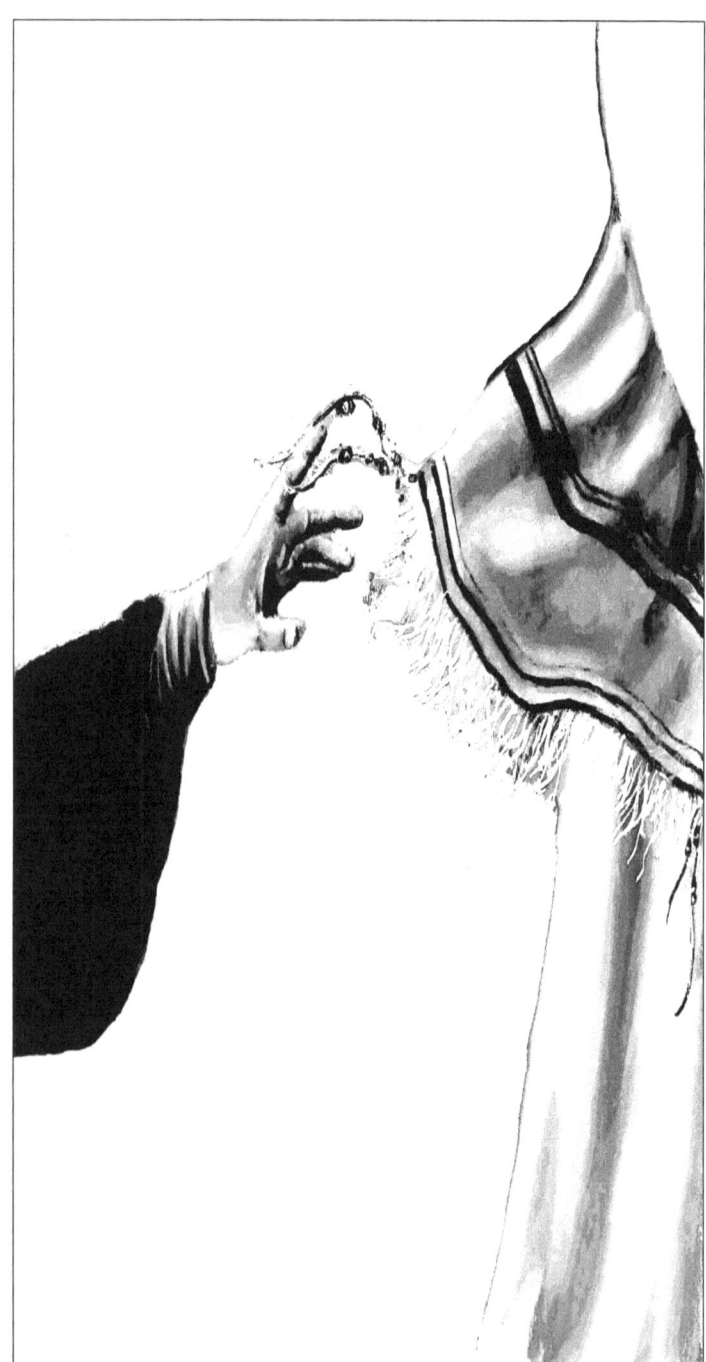

What People Are Saying About This Book

"Having read the beautiful and poetic prayers Mrs. Pandya has written, I can tell you it is like opening up the book of Psalms. So rich, you know instantly, she has poured her heart out upon the page. There is no doubt, the Spirit of God dwells within her and speaks to her, as she writes. It's been a privilege and a blessing to read."

—Ann Plymale
Preschool Director
Northwood Church
Keller, Texas

"Don't just read the poems in this book but know that each poem has an anointing of love and gratitude to our great God. Each poem is written from the deepest part of the heart and one could not stop but lift up the holy hands to worship while reading this book of psalms and poetry."

I wonder if this is what God meant when He prophesied through the prophet that, He will raise the fallen tabernacle of David in the last day. I kept thinking that this should be labeled "Psalms of Vini."

—Janet Martin
Office of the Prophet
The Harvest Church
Thornton, Colorado

"Vini Pandya writes from her heart. As you read this book, her faith, love, and trust in the Lord, will minister to you."

—Alph Samuel, Pastor,
Gateway Church,
Dallas, Texas

"I have had the privilege of knowing Vini Pandya for many years and over this time I have seen her great love for the Lord Jesus Christ expressed in every area of her life. This book of Poems lays bare the real and heartfelt journey of a true worshiper and takes us into the depths of knowing the one who is her beloved.

It is a beautiful expression of love for our magnificent God, despite the challenges, griefs and trials encountered by Vini. I believe that the Savior's touch of emotional and spiritual healing is upon these poems and I am sure that they will be a blessing to all who read them."

—Carolyn Penna,
Hillsong Church,
Sydney, Australia

"Tears streamed down my face as I finished reading the final reflection of this book. All throughout this book of poems, every word points back to the faithfulness and love of God and how His presence captivates our hearts. I am grateful for the privilege to have been asked to read it."

—Dalenea Myers,
Fort Worth, TX

Copyright © 2020 Vandana Tejas Pandya
ISBN: 9781698673806
Library of Congress Control Number: 2019919727
Published in the United States of America

All rights reserved as permitted under the U. S. Copyright Act of 1976. No part of this publication may be reproduced, distributed, or transmitted in any form or by any means, or stored in a database or retrieval system, without the expressed written permission of the author and publisher.

Unless otherwise identified, all Scripture quotations have been taken from *THE HOLY BIBLE, NEW INTERNATIONAL VERSION*®, NIV® Copyright © 1973, 1978, 1984, 2011 by Biblica, Inc.® Used by permission. All rights reserved worldwide.

Scripture quotations marked NLT are taken from the *Holy Bible, New Living Translation*, copyright © 1996, 2004, 2015 by Tyndale House Foundation. Used by permission of Tyndale House Publishers, Inc., Carol Stream, Illinois 60188. Used by permission. All rights reserved.

Scripture quotations marked ESV are taken from *The ESV® Bible* (*The Holy Bible, English Standard Version®*). Copyright © 2001 by Crossway, a publishing ministry of Good News Publishers. Used by permission. All rights reserved.

Published in association with

&

Bedford , Texas
www.BurkhartBooks.com

Dedication

I Touched The Hem Of His Garment is dedicated to the lover of my soul and the first love of my life my Lord and Savior Jesus Christ.

This book of poetry is a little glimpse into the beauty and majesty of a great Architect and Builder of life. Every poem has been inspired by the living Word of God.

God the Father, who is a life-giver, gave us our Prince of Peace, Jesus Christ. And Jesus Christ, the life-saver gave us our life-guide, the precious Holy Spirit.

I encourage the readers to enjoy the love of the Lord and to see themselves as truly the children of the Most High God.

I humble myself and with a heartfelt gratitude want to convey to the world that once we let Jesus hold our hands, we will get through life with immense joy and an unexplainable peace no matter what the circumstances.

Please join me in this journey of praising and loving our Savior …

A Word Of Thanks

As I write this book, my heart is full of gratitude for my life. I am where I am today simply by the grace and loving kindness of our God. He has blessed me with a loving family; wonderful parents, a lovely sister, an amazing husband, and my more than precious children. I consider myself the Lord's highly favored one! He has given me a lot to be thankful for.

I want to sincerely thank various Christian ministers and ministries around the world for sending out the Word and for the encouragement they have provided over the years. They have been instrumental in influencing and shaping my life with their nuggets of Godly wisdom.

I started my journey as a believer of the Lord Jesus Christ in India when I had a vision of a burning Cross in my room. This led me to a small fellowship of believers called Masih Mandali. Few months later, I moved to another city, and was baptized at the Living Hope Church. I learned the basic fundamentals of faith and attended Bible study at Delhi Bible Fellowship and then moved to New Life Fellowship for which I am eternally grateful.

After moving to Dubai, I joined a Filipino evangelical congregation called KNB, which left a deep influence on my life. King's Revival Church International was a huge blessing that helped me grow on another level in my faith.

In 2008, I got married and moved to Sydney, Australia, and had the privilege of being a part of the Hillsong Church and the Christian City Church, both of which are anointed places of worship. We are thankful for the various friends and Godly saints that we have crossed paths with.

Moving to the United States was nothing short of God's divine plan for us. We are thankful for the prayer hub at the International Community Church; friends at Church of South India in Dallas, Texas and now we are so blessed to be planted at the Gateway Church in Dallas, Texas.

Thank you everyone for being a part of my journey!

Acknowledgments

I want to thank and acknowledge certain people who have been instrumental in making this book possible. I believe they are the saints that God put on my path to remove the stumbling blocks and they have been a huge support in my journey.

I am so grateful for Ms Laura Grund, Rev V S Bhandari, Ms Elizabeth Samuel, Mr Kushal Jung Thapa, Ms Carolyn Penna and Ms Sakshi Kapoor for their valuable contributions.

I am ever grateful for my husband Mr. Tejas Pandya who has completely supported me every step of the way. My sweet children have contributed by praying their hearts out to God for this book to touch people's lives in a spectacular life altering way.

Still others who have touched my life in ways that left a deep impact on my life and it all came in the form of experiences while writing this book of songs and poetry.

Content

What People Are Saying About This Book
Dedication
A Word Of Thanks
Acknowledgments
Foreword 15
I Touched The Hem Of His Garment 17

1. Arms Open Wide 19
2. Church 21
3. Communion Song 23
4. Father, Spirit, Son 25
5. Father Turned His Face Away 29
6. For The Sake Of Love 33
7. Grant Me My Heart's Desire 37
8. He Will Hold Your Hand Forever 39
9. Holy Spirit Sung 43
10. I Am Your Holy Temple 45
11. I Believe Lord, Help My Unbelief 49
12. I Dared Open My Sword 51
13. I Touched The Hem Of His Garment: Part 1 53
14. I Touched The Hem Of His Garment: Part 2 57
15. I Wonder, How It's Gonna Be! 59
16. May None Be Left Behind, I Pray 63
17. Me, A Mother ... 65
18. My Testimony 67
19. One With You 71
20. Praise Song 73
21. Redeem The Time and Honor The Sabbath 75
22. Revival 79
23. Savior To Me Is No Other 83
24. Say "No" To The World, If You Wanna Say "Yes" To God 85
25. Seated On The Highest Throne 87
26. Shalom 89

27.	Son Of Man	91
28.	Sound Of Rain	95
29.	Take My Heart Lord, And Hide It Inside Yours	97
30.	The Blood	99
31.	The Lamb Slain For Me, The Lion Who Paid For Me	103
32.	The Light And The Salt	107
33.	The Resurrection	109
34.	Time And Time Again	113
35.	Water My Soul	117
36.	Who Do You Say I Am?	119
37:	Yeshua - The Light Of The World	123

I Touched The Hem Of His Garment And Healing He Gave To Me …	127
Sharing My Heart …	131

About The Author

Foreword

"Vini Pandya's book is as powerful as the title. When the woman who needed healing touched the garment of Jesus, a power transaction happened. The woman was healed immediately and Jesus knew that power had come out of Him and knew He was touched. This book gives us the ability to reach out and touch God and receive the power of God through poetry.

Vini Pandya has successfully captured the heart of God for His people in a profoundly beautiful way. Her poems are thought provoking, emotionally moving, and open our eyes to a deep and intimate love that Jesus has for each one of us.

This book of poetry is highly recommended for anyone looking for a deeper connection with God or for those wanting to learn more about who He is and how He truly sees and feels about us."

—Scott Venable
Lead Pastor
Northwood Church,
Keller, TX

I touched the hem of His garment

A large crowd followed and pressed around him. And a woman was there who had been subject to bleeding for twelve years. She had suffered a great deal under the care of many doctors and had spent all she had, yet instead of getting better she grew worse. When she heard about Jesus, she came up behind him in the crowd and touched his cloak, because she thought, "If I just touch his clothes, I will be healed." Immediately her bleeding stopped and she felt in her body that she was freed from her suffering.

At once Jesus realized that power had gone out from him. He turned around in the crowd and asked, "Who touched my clothes?"

"You see the people crowding against you," his disciples answered, "and yet you can ask, 'Who touched me?'"

But Jesus kept looking around to see who had done it. Then the woman, knowing what had happened to her, came and fell at his feet and, trembling with fear, told him the whole truth. He said to her, "Daughter, your faith has healed you. Go in peace and be freed from your suffering."

Mark 5:24-34

Living Word of God
Sharper than any double~edged sword

Revelation 3:20

Here I am! I stand at the door and knock. If anyone hears my voice and opens the door, I will come in and eat with that person, and they with me.

Luke 19:9

Jesus said to him, "Today salvation has come to this house, because this man, too, is a son of Abraham.

1. Arms Open Wide

I stand at the door and knock,
For you to open up your heart!
With a gentle whisper,
I call your name.
Let the Spirit prompt your heart!
Do not fear and now unlock
The door of your heart,
Way too long, that has been locked!
I'll show you a better way,
Than any human mind could say!
Let your king of glory come in,
To dine with you
For a life of feast!
Hold on tight,
For salvation has come today,
With arms open wide!

Living Word of God
Sharper than any double~edged sword

Matthew 16:18

… and on this rock I will build my church, and the gates of Hades will not overcome it.

Psalm 69:9

… zeal for your house consumes me …

John 21:16

Again Jesus said, "Simon son of John, do you love me?" He answered, "Yes, Lord, you know that I love you." Jesus said, "Take care of my sheep."

2. Church

Church is a place where God is magnified,
A place where Truth is highlighted,
And God's laws are highly respected,
A place where young and old are welcome and accepted,
And are made to feel delighted,
Where your friendship with the Lord is expected,
And forgiveness & love is genuinely practiced,
Where saints are to The Holy Spirit attracted.
And there is freedom to worship & obey,
Where The Potter molds the clay.
It's a place of love and care,
Where they come and happily share.
Standing up for each other,
They bear another's burden.
The Gospel Truth we learn deeper,
As one has promised to be another's keeper.
Where passion for God's house is strong and evident,
Where they serve, they sing, they laugh,
They play, they do it all together.
Cause the call they obey,
Is of the highest order,
Where Jesus is The Shepherd,
And the sheep, they must obey!

LIVING WORD OF GOD
SHARPER THAN ANY DOUBLE~EDGED SWORD

Luke 22:19-20

… *"This is my body given for you; do this in remembrance of me."*
… *"This cup is the new covenant in my blood, which is poured out for you …"*

3. Communion Song

Eat the bread and drink the wine
Sing praises to my Lord my God
He is King over all I tell you
He is King over all

Most powerful God is He
Jesus is His name
He gave His life for me
I am gonna praise His Holy name

Come on all you people come on
Clap your hands and praise
Raise the banner high I tell you
He is Son of God

He died for me
He rose up from the grave
He is perfect Lamb of God
Jesus is His name

Thank Him from your heart I tell you
Praise His Holy name
Jesus is the son of God
And Jesus is my all

Eat the bread and drink the wine
Sing praises to my Lord my God
He is King over all I tell you
He is King over all

LIVING WORD OF GOD
SHARPER THAN ANY DOUBLE~EDGED SWORD

Luke 1:35

… The Holy Spirit will come on you, and the power of the Most High will overshadow you. So the Holy One to be born will be called the Son of God.

John 6:51

I am the living bread that came down from heaven. Whoever eats this bread will live forever. This bread is my flesh, which I will give for the life of the world.

4. Father, Spirit, Son

Father, Spirit, Son, connect me to yourself,
Father, Spirit, Son, connect me to yourself,

Lord I know I am, just a tiny one,
Lord I know You are, greater than anyone.

Still my Lord, my God,
There's a longing in my heart!

Though You are my Lord,
I know that in my heart.

Still my heart is craving,
For Your presence more and more!

How sweet are You my Lord,
You're the Savior of the world.

You led me all these years,
And brought me so very far.

I know you are my Lord,
You are the "Living Bread."

You've cleansed me, O my Lord,
With the drops of Your blood.

I Touched The Hem Of His Garment

You've made a way to heaven,
For all who've come to You.

You've freed us from our sins,
No matter what we did.

You are my God, my Savior,
I'll bless Your name forever!

Thank you, O my Lord,
For paying the price you did!

You are the Lord of heaven,
Yet, so close to me.

How wonderful You are,
Wish I could touch and see!

The glory of the Lord,
That's holy and supreme!

Hallelujah, to Your name,
You are my Lord, my God.

Thank You for the privilege,
I have everything in You.

My soul is satisfied,
'Cause God I am one with You.

LIVING WORD OF GOD
SHARPER THAN ANY DOUBLE~EDGED SWORD

Matthew 26:39

"… My Father, if it is possible, may this cup be taken from me. Yet not as I will, but as you will."

John 3:16

For God so loved the world that he gave his one and only Son, that whoever believes in him shall not perish but have eternal life.

5. Father Turned His Face Away

It was in the Garden of Gethsemane,
Those early morning hours,
Where He knelt down to pray.

I wonder how restless His soul must've been.
How much pain and grief to bear.

And there was no one with whom He could openly share.
Sure, there was doubt and pain of the coming betrayal.

I guess there was fear and maybe some tears.
The reason He came for, that hour was near.
The purpose was being met, at the cost of His breath!

Still for a moment, how He wished an escape!
When to His Father, He whispered and prayed,
If the cup of suffering could simply pass by,
Still not His will, but the Father's be done.

The pain, the shame, the suffering and disgrace
    all had come together,
Mocking in His forgiving face, nothing to hold dear.

Sure, it grieved the Father's heart,
More than the words could ever say.

Thinking of His only Son,
And of the soldiers ready to slay.

Yet it was for your good and mine,
That Father turned His face away.

LIVING WORD OF GOD
SHARPER THAN ANY DOUBLE~EDGED SWORD

Psalm 139:14

I praise you because I am fearfully and wonderfully made; your works are wonderful, I know that full well.

6. For The Sake Of Love

To My Lord and Savior Jesus Christ:

My Righteous One, My Holy One,
The Sacred One, The Exalted One.

Though, thousands and thousands of years may pass,
You, O Lord are going to be The Only One.

The Unchanging One, The Ever Living One,
The Lord of hosts, The Lord of the lost.

Calling me by my name,
Making me Your very own.

My Shepherd God, My all in all,
My greatest victory, My strongest virtue.

My Friend in need, my Friend indeed,
My health may fail, my own may disown,

The tide may pass, the winds may blow,
On my face and give me a blow,

You will hold me, so very tight
That all I fear, is losing Your sight.

Nothing can shake, nothing can break,
The faith You've given, will sustain.

Help me endure, the toughest journey,
the roughest ride.

All for Your glory I will stand,
For You will see me to the end.

Your creation, Your admiration,
Work of Your hands, Your imagination.

Shining in the brightest light,
I am Yours and You are mine.

One day the journey on earth will be over,
When I will cross the shore and come over.

In Your sight and in Your presence,
To my home that is called heaven,

I am assured,
there You'll be present.

You'll be glad, to see me my King,
You'll adorn me with the Heavenly ring.

Till my days on earth, are not yet over,
You'll grace me with the faith I need,
And strengthen me for the walk I have.

I will stand and proclaim,
The Mighty Name, the Sacred Name,
The Worthy Name, the Matchless Name.
Name so dear,
That generates reverent fear.

To my friends who are listening and still deciding:

He is near, if you hear,
Still calling you by name,
Wanting to make you
His very own.
Don't take so long my friend,
Before you decide,
The end might come!

Living Word of God
Sharper than any double~edged sword

Ephesians 4:32

Be kind and compassionate to one another, forgiving each other, just as in Christ God forgave you.

7. Grant Me My Heart's Desire

The small desire of my heart,
Is to please You my King!
When You show me mercy Lord,
Teach me to pass it all along!
When I seek Your forgiveness,
Let me forgive the ones who've hurt!
When I seek Your love for me,
Let me love the way You loved!
When I ask You to bless me Lord,
Let me bless the ones You love!
When I seek Your healing Lord,
Let my words may never wound!
When I pray before You Lord,
Let Your ears always hear!
When in Your kingdom I may enter,
Let Your eyes be upon me, my King!
When my life is at the end,
I will wait for You my friend!
When You come to take me home,
Please bless my earthly friends!

Living Word of God
Sharper than any double~edged sword

Genesis 3:9

The Lord God called to the man, "Where are you?

Romans 8:28

And we know that in all things God works for the good of those who love him, who have been called according to his purpose.

8. He Will Hold Your Hand Forever

In the midst of our busyness,
When our God came looking,
We were too occupied to pay Him any heed,
As we were all trying to meet our daily needs.

He sent many signals, He sent us His longings,
He tried to remind us, in many forms and ways,
But His gentle soft voice got mixed amongst
    too many voices.
His heart started grieving, as we all made our choices.

None of us was ready, none of us was willing,
To go the extra mile that was truly filling.
We all stayed hungry, we all starved our souls,
Our outsides looked attractive, our insides lacked
    the source.

We took too much on our plates, none to satisfy,
But to show to others, what a player am I!
Our hungry souls still unfulfilled, craving and
    thirsting to fill the longings only God could satisfy.
Should wandering aimlessly we die?

Did not all things He worked for our good?
Did He not command the storms to stop
And the blind to see?
Did not the plagues of blood & frogs, lice & flies,
    livestock pestilence,

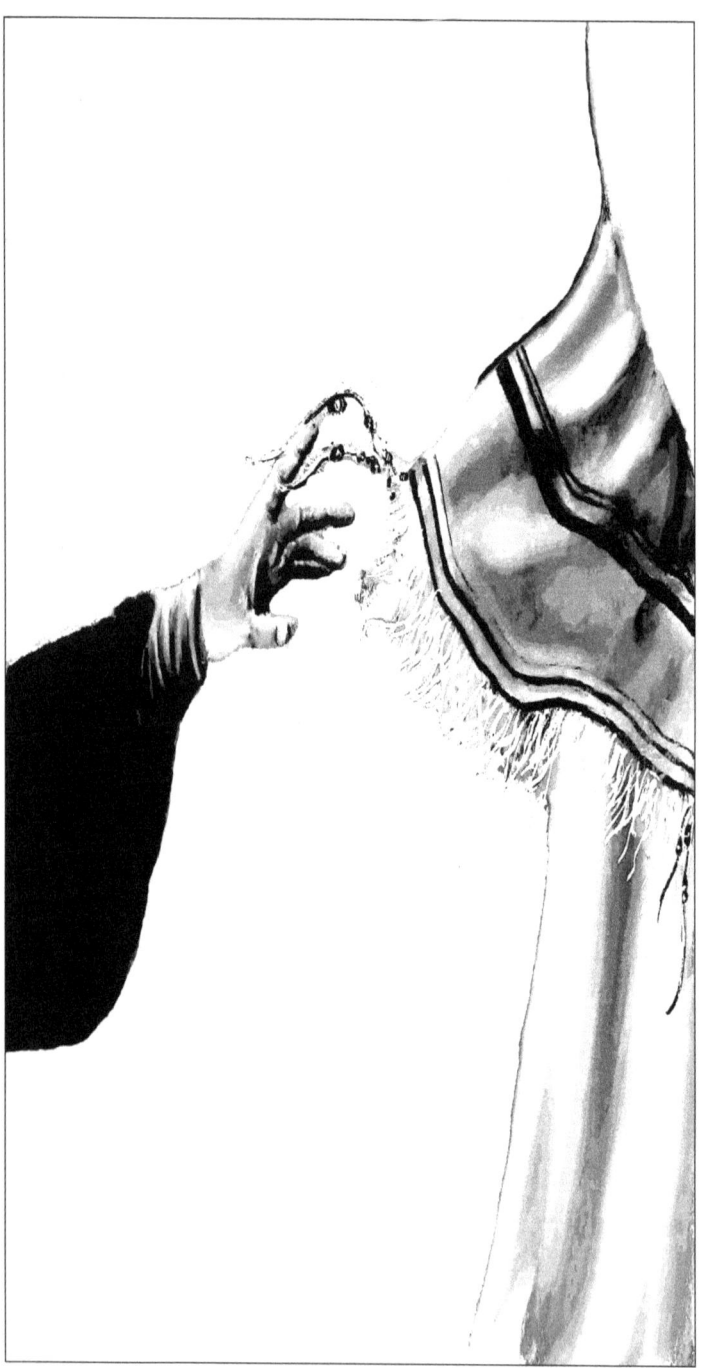

I Touched The Hem Of His Garment

Boils & hail, locusts & darkness and even the killing of
   the babes was
His plan to rescue your soul and mine?

God intervened in the past when His creation could
   not identify,
His plans and purposes were all going to unify,
When His thoughts and desires to rescue and redeem
   His Sovereign Kingdom came by,
And all of the heavens shook and earth quaked and
   gave way.

When His only Son hung on that wooden Cross,
To His Father that was His biggest loss,
Yet in His dying eyes across, it was your face and mine
   He saw,
Which made it easy for Him to let His precious Son go!

What makes you wonder, "this time He won't
   come through?"
He is the God of covenant, who stood up for you.
He Who is true to His Word, Can He deny Himself?
He will hold your hand forever, though your promise
   to Him may not be true!

(Written at the time when the world pandemic of 2020 was at its peak)

Living Word of God
Sharper than any double~edged sword

Psalm 98:1

Sing to the LORD a new song, for he has done marvelous things …

Romans 8:26

… the Spirit helps us in our weakness. We do not know what we ought to pray for, but the Spirit himself intercedes for us through wordless groans.

9. Holy Spirit Sung

The Holy Spirit of God,
Put a song in my heart.
Languages unknown to me,
But so much in tune,
Yet, not for me to understand!
I don't remember the lyrics,
And have forgotten all those words.
All I recollect is that,
My heart was all praising and tears filled my eyes.
The Lord's name, was all that was being glorified,
The Lord's name, was all that was being magnified,
The Lord's servant was terrified, at the sight …
That she was qualified, to serve her Master
    and her King.
Who gave her this privilege? She thought to herself…
Is she even worthy, to untie the thongs of His sandals?
It was then, the gentle whisper of the Lord, rang into
    her ears …
"You my darling, are my precious possession.
I shed My blood, to buy your happiness,
I love to see you smile,
Don't ever cry, why do you cry?
Now, you don't have to die.
I have carved your name, on the palm of My hand,
I won't ever let you sigh.
I have lived, so shall you live and serve at
    My temple courts."

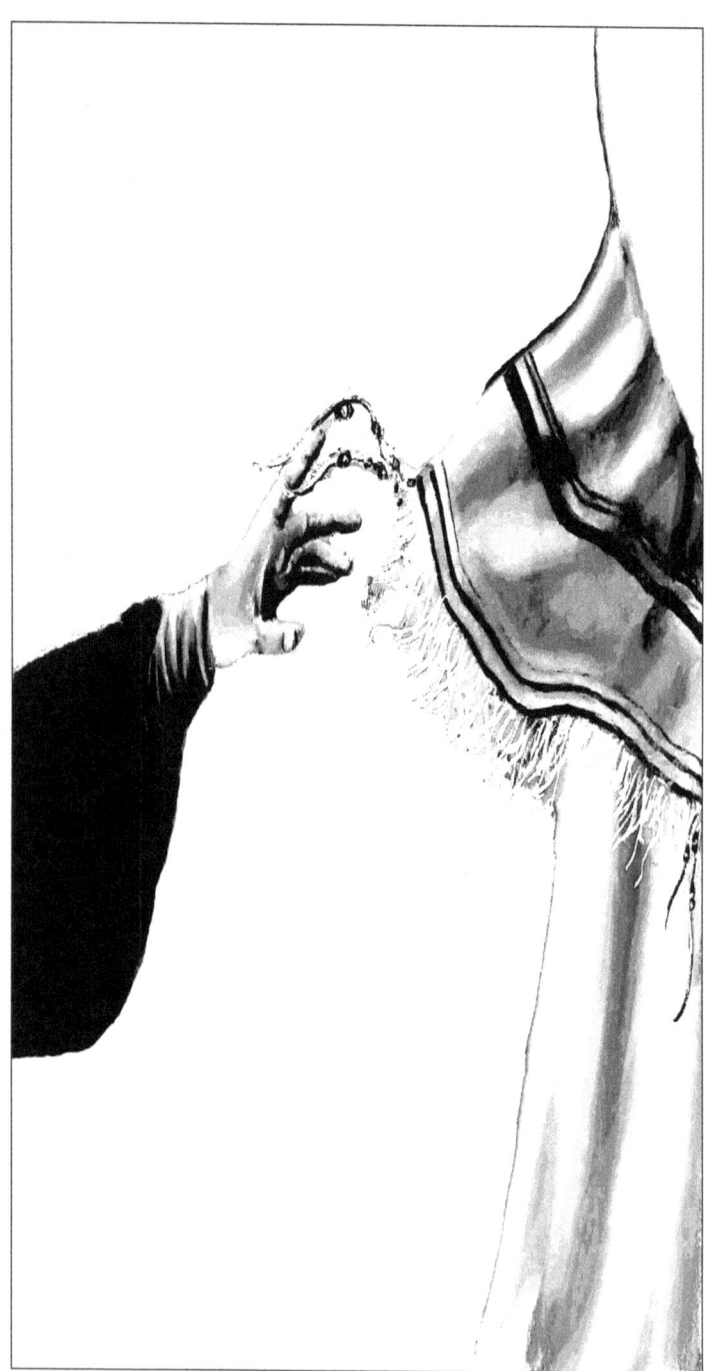

Wow! What a privilege it was for her to bask in His unending presence.
What a privilege it is, to be called the friend of the Most High!

Living Word of God
Sharper than any double~edged sword

1 Corinthians 6:19-20

Do you not know that your bodies are temples of the Holy Spirit, who is in you, whom you have received from God? You are not your own; you were bought at a price. Therefore honor God with your bodies.

10. I Am Your Holy Temple

I am Your holy temple,
Since You dwell in me.
O my sweet Savior,
Let me rest & abide in Thee.
In You I find that place of rest,
In You my heart is at its best.
You cause me to glorify Thy name,
For Your glory to rise and shine,
Through my life, that's now divine.
Show Your mercy in my life,
And gain the victory over my mind.
This life be used for purpose bright,
And never again cause me to doubt.
My love for You,
May always cry out!

Living Word of God
Sharper than any double~edged sword

Mark 9:23-24

… Everything is possible for one who believes.

11. I Believe Lord, Help My Unbelief

Answer Lord, O Answer Lord,
Once again, my prayer,
Folding my hands, I come,
With a heart that still believes.

You alone are the fire, Lord,
That can brighten up my day.
Though I walk through the stony path,
Your light will show me the way.

I cry out to you my Lord,
For You alone can heal,
You can heal, and You can peel,
Every layer of unbelief.

Restorer You are,
Redeemer, they call You,
You can restore and You can redeem,
My faith in Christ Jesus again.

LIVING WORD OF GOD
SHARPER THAN ANY DOUBLE~EDGED SWORD

Hebrews 4:12

For the word of God is alive and active. Sharper than any double-edged sword, it penetrates even to dividing soul and spirit, joints and marrow; it judges the thoughts and attitudes of the heart.

12. I Dared Open My Sword

Father, Father I call You my Lord,
As I dared open my Sword.

My eyes on the beauty of those words as I lay,
Though wrapped in majesty and kingdom;
You chose for them; to You they slay.

The Truth forgotten, the King ill-gotten,
Massacred and drilled, there Your body lay,
All for us sinners, the big price You must pay.

Filled me with pain, of what remained,
Sad to hear, that You had been blamed,
When it was I, who was meant to pay,
The price eternal, for the cross of the criminal.

Still when the love, in Your eyes I see,
I fall at your feet, with one single plea,
That my heart may find a place in Thee.

Living Word of God
Sharper than any double~edged sword

Matthew 9:20-21

Just then a woman who had been subject to bleeding for twelve years came up behind him and touched the edge of his cloak. She said to herself, "If I only touch his cloak, I will be healed."

13. I Touched The Hem Of His Garment: Part 1

I touched the hem of His garment,
And power flowed upon me,

The Lord in all His fullness,
Is revealing His glory to me,

O I cannot fathom,
My eyes cannot see,

Such a bright radiance,
Of the Lord God Almighty!

He defeated the enemy,
And won the victory,

And forever,
He set me free.

The serpent was,
So wicked and crafty,

Deceiving the world,
By his magic and charm,

I Touched The Hem Of His Garment

But in front of my Lord,
Even he could not stand,

For the blood of the Lamb,
Is my refuge and balm!

I walk in victory,
Because of what my Savior has done for me,

He paid in full,
And settled my case,

He delivered me,
From death and curse,

He promised me,
A crowning life,

His blood was shed,
And I came up from the mud.

Living Word of God
Sharper than any double~edged sword

Psalm 89:9 ESV

You rule the raging of the sea; when its waves rise, you still them.

2 Cor. 1:21-22

… He anointed us, set his seal of ownership on us, and put his Spirit in our hearts as a deposit, guaranteeing what is to come.

14. I Touched The Hem Of His Garment: Part 2

I touched the hem of His garment,
And healing He gave to me.

With trembling voice and fearful eyes,
As I approached my Savior,

In royal attire, there He stood,
Calming the raging sea.

The Savior healed, as I leaned,
With His blood, He made me clean.

His power flowed and overflowed,
So much so, that He wouldn't let go.

Called me His own, gave me His peace,
He put on me, His ownership seal.

Now I belong to the Heavenly King,
And so, His praises, I will always sing.

LIVING WORD OF GOD
SHARPER THAN ANY DOUBLE~EDGED SWORD

Revelation 1:8

"I am the Alpha and the Omega," says the Lord God, "who is, and who was, and who is to come, the Almighty."

15. I Wonder, How It's Gonna Be!

When I see my Lord face to face,
I wonder, "How it's gonna be!"
His heart's white & pure,
And mine's dark & shabby.
Yet, He is full of grace,
And abounds Himself in love.
Though I sinned all my life,
And cried day & night.
His hope's still on me,
That one day I'll come home.
What a loving Father,
Who gives another chance!
If my God hadn't been on my side,
I wonder where I'd be!
So, let the glory of the Lord be revealed,
To all the earth I say.
Let my King who's full of grace and mercy,
May rule His kingdom night and day.
May all His flocks obey Him;
And love Him with all they are!
As the light of the Lord,
Reaches the ends of the earth,
The darkness dims,
As truth prevails.
Alpha and Omega, He proclaims to be,
From everlasting to everlasting, our God is He.

Yes, He is God of all the earth,
Yet so kind and pure.
Who is like the Lord my God?
No one, but Him alone,
Who paid for my every sin,
At the cost of His dying breath.
He lives and He reigns,
Today and every day.
Come on, all you people come on,
Lift your hands and pray.

LIVING WORD OF GOD
SHARPER THAN ANY DOUBLE~EDGED SWORD

Matthew 24:40-42

Two men will be in the field; one will be taken and the other left. Two women will be grinding with a hand mill; one will be taken and the other left.

"Therefore keep watch, because you do not know on what day your Lord will come."

16. May None Be Left Behind, I Pray

God of mercy, God of love,
Your name be honored,
Your name be loved!
You promised to come one day,
When one be taken,
And one will stay!
The one who follows,
Won't go astray!
And on that sacred day,
When from Your judgment seat You judge,
Mercy may shower, sin may shun!
All be taken, none may stay,
Cry of my heart,
May none be left behind,
I pray!

LIVING WORD OF GOD
SHARPER THAN ANY DOUBLE~EDGED SWORD

Psalm 127:3

Children are a heritage from the Lord, offspring a reward from him.

Isaiah 40:11

He tends his flock like a shepherd:
He gathers the lambs in his arms
and carries them close to his heart;
he gently leads those that have young.

17. Me, A Mother ...

Thank you for the privilege Father,
To bear Your sons and daughters.
Carry them in my womb for You,
And give them food and water.
Love and care for them, like I cared for no other!
Watch them as they learn and grow, in wisdom
    and in stature,
Be more patient with them, as they learn the shapes
    and colors,
Teach them, as they learn to be better than each other,
Stand by them, when they learn to keep their hearts
    pure and clear,
Correct them, when they choose to go the path that
    has all glitters,
Be a friend to them, when they need to talk and share.
You have shown that faith in me, that I can be
    their mother.
Let my life may be to them, a treasure that
    they can share!

Living Word of God
Sharper than any double~edged sword

John 14:6

Jesus answered, "I am the way and the truth and the life. No one comes to the Father except through me.

Ephesians 2:8-9

For it is by grace you have been saved, through faith—and this is not from yourselves, it is the gift of God—not by works, so that no one can boast.

18. My Testimony

I was searching for Truth,
There was deep hollowness inside of me.

I was wrestling, I was struggling,
For God to show Himself to me!

My nights were almost sleepless,
My days were also sad.

Bitterness was surrounding me,
No rest was upon me.

I was craving for something,
To be revealed to me.

I could not imagine the grace,
He was pouring on me,

That one day, the Lord had mercy on me,
He chose to reveal His glory to me!

What I saw, was not a man, nor a woman,
Or any statue or any form.

It was the Cross that was burning,
And light flowed upon me!

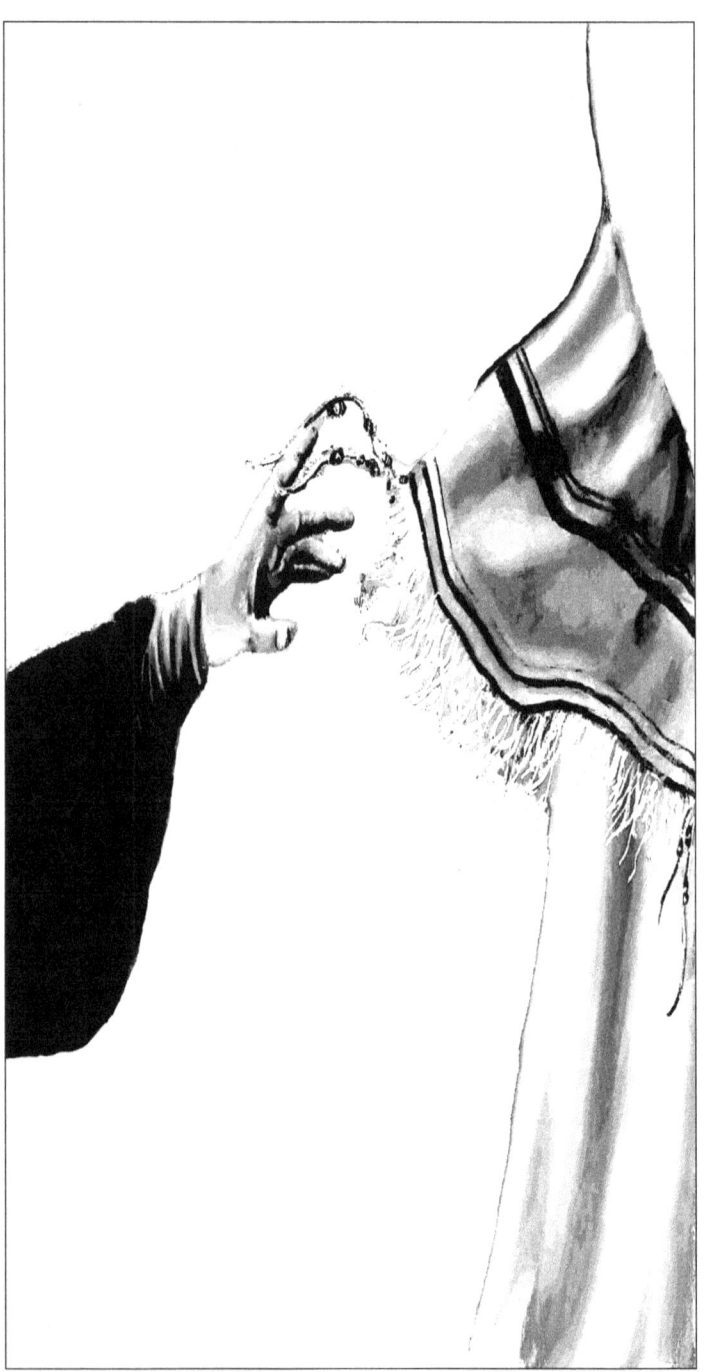

What a beautiful vision,
The Lord had shown to me.

I sit and I think,
About that moment again...!

That was just the beginning of something so beautiful,
He had in store for me!

I am still craving for more of His presence,
To flow through me!

Because His love is a deep ocean,
Which takes care of me.

LIVING WORD OF GOD
SHARPER THAN ANY DOUBLE~EDGED SWORD

Jeremiah 20:9

… His word is in my heart like a fire, a fire shut up in my bones …

19. One With You

You are the Lord that I will seek,
You are the Lord that always heals.
Seek You with all my heart,
Praise You with all I am.
Reaching to Your secret place,
Calling out Your holy name.
Your Word on my heart,
Like fire burning all my bones.
I will praise and meditate,
In You alone I saturate.
So much so, my heart be one,
I'll join it with the Holy One.
Never to separate again,
Always in Your love remain.

Living Word of God
Sharper than any double~edged sword

Psalm 150:1-5

Praise God in His sanctuary;
  Praise Him in His mighty heavens.
Praise Him for His acts of power;
  Praise Him for His surpassing greatness.
Praise Him with the sounding of the trumpet,
  Praise Him with the harp and lyre,
Praise Him with timbrel and dancing,
  Praise Him with the strings and pipe,
Praise Him with the clash of cymbals,
  Praise Him with resounding cymbals.

20. Praise Song

Lord would you let me praise Your Holy name,
Lord would you let me sit down at Your feet,
Lord would you let me kiss Your gentle face,
Lord would you let me bask in Your grace!

Oh, as the time goes,
Oh, my Lord.
I am reminded of Your precious love.

You gave Your All for me,
You gave Your Soul,
You gave Your Life for me,
You gave Your Whole.

What a sacrifice Lord, all done for me,
What a life You led Lord, example for me.

You are my Redeemer,
You are my Friend.
May I follow, may I follow,
You to the end!

Living Word of God
Sharper than any double-edged sword

Exodus 20:8-11

Remember the Sabbath day by keeping it holy. Six days you shall labor and do all your work, but the seventh day is a sabbath to the Lord your God. On it you shall not do any work, neither you, nor your son or daughter, nor your male or female servant, nor your animals, nor any foreigner residing in your towns. For in six days the Lord made the heavens and the earth, the sea, and all that is in them, but he rested on the seventh day. Therefore the Lord blessed the Sabbath day and made it holy ....

21. Redeem The Time: Come To The Table And Honor The Sabbath

Do not waste it, do not fight it,
This time you've been given is a gift in disguise.
You don't see it, you don't feel it,
It's truly a sign from the Holy Divine.

You've been given new task to do,
Sit in His presence and love Him anew,
He has waited long enough,
He's not surprised, you are still not through!

Come and make a sanctuary,
Let Him be your primary,
Rest of the world is temporary,
He alone is your eternity.

The time to hustle and the time to bustle,
Has come to a still, just do not wrestle,
For the world it may seem like a puzzle,
But sitting by His side, it all feels like a drizzle.

The wind has blown and the tide has turned,
Very soon will the world return,
Seasons are changing, fast approaching,
Feed your soul, while you are in the waiting.

I Touched The Hem Of His Garment

Tomorrow when you look back,
You'll have stories all stacked,
People who had all their lives mapped,
Are suddenly feeling so very sad.

The time to sow and the time to reap,
Has come to a place, where all will weep.
Weeping and gnashing has filled the earth,
Yet in times of redemption, the enemy is crushed.

So light the candles and welcome The King,
In His presence you may dance and sing,
Read the Word and keep the sabbath,
Bless the Lord and blow the shofar.

Eat the bread and drink the wine,
Gather your people to eat and dine.
It's His grace that carries you fine,
Let His face on you may shine.

(Written in the midst of the world pandemic of 2020)

Living Word of God
Sharper than any double~edged sword

Luke 15:31-32

"My son," the father said, "you are always with me, and everything I have is yours. But we had to celebrate and be glad, because this brother of yours was dead and is alive again; he was lost and is found."

22. Revival

Let the revival come in this place,
If only they may know and seek His holy face.

The voice of my King, in their hearts may take seed,
As it reaches to the millions in need.

Oh, how I wish, for you to get saved,
For your name in the book of heaven to get engraved.

May your light shine, O my friend,
As you let Him guide you, to the end.

There is hope till His mercy dawns,
There is light till His grace abounds.

He wants forever, to be your guide,
Only if you let Him be by your side.

He promises to cover your darkest side,
Provided, you let Him wipe that inner pride.

Solely by His blood, can you and I,
Live that life, that truly satisfy.

I am amazed, how each time they cry,
Folding their hands, in prayer they lay.

I Touched The Hem Of His Garment

His eyes go looking,
His arms outstretched,

Running He goes,
Longing to embrace,

The repentant sinner,
His precious one,

The chosen son,
Who once got lost in the crowd.

What a joy he now brought,
To his Father's delight,

And has become
His Father's pride.

LIVING WORD OF GOD
SHARPER THAN ANY DOUBLE~EDGED SWORD

1 John 4:14

And we have seen and testify that the Father has sent his Son to be the Savior of the world.

23. Savior To Me Is No Other

You grew in wisdom and in stature,
To break all the rules regulations,
You healed the man on the Sabbath,
You peeled the old so-called record,
You made well the bleeding women,
Changed her to be Your spokesperson,
When on the wedding, the wine You gave,
To Your mother, such pride You gave,
When to Lazarus You called,
Thy courageous act was applaud,
You showed Your power and Your glory,
That was all written like a story,
For all to read and embrace,
If they want to enjoy the grace,
Loving are Your ways forever,
Teaching wisdom to the clever,
Holiness is Your golden rule,
Making all those tempers cool,
You alone are the Healer,
No one can wash my sins cleaner,
Once abandoned by Thy Father,
Savior to me is no other.

Living Word of God
Sharper than any double~edged sword

Matthew 16:24-26

Then Jesus said to his disciples, "Whoever wants to be my disciple must deny themselves and take up their cross and follow me. For whoever wants to save their life will lose it, but whoever loses their life for me will find it. What good will it be for someone to gain the whole world, yet forfeit their soul? Or what can anyone give in exchange for their soul?

24. Say "No" To The World, If You Wanna Say "Yes" To God

To walk with God is a price too high.
You ought to pay it if you wanna fly high.
The blood of my Savior is way too high.
You cannot mess around, and you cannot also lie.
If you know, you are bought with His blood,
Your price is also high.
You don't know, what you are worth,
If you still are playing around.
You can't steal any longer,
You can't covet any further.
God who is your Savior,
Is pleading with you my friend.
The oil He poured on you
Is the most expensive product of Heaven.
He paid His all,
Whatever He had in His share,
'Cause He wanted to show,
How much He loved and cared!

Living Word of God
Sharper than any double~edged sword

Matthew 28:20

... Surely I am with you always, to the very end of the age.

25. Seated On The Highest Throne

Seated on the highest throne,
Judging the world with fairness and love,
The greatest Emperor of all times,
One who was, and is, and is to come.
My seat in heaven is secured,
Of that I am assured,
Not because I am perfect,
But because my King suffered.
I am now debt free,
'Cause my Rescuer set me free.
The penalty that He paid,
Caused Him shame and utter disgrace.
Yet He leads, as He pleads,
For your sake and mine, He bleeds.
What a great leader He is,
To whom He leads, to them He feeds.
Never will He leave His sheep,
That's the promise for you & I to keep.

LIVING WORD OF GOD
SHARPER THAN ANY DOUBLE~EDGED SWORD

John 14:27

Peace I leave with you; my peace I give you. I do not give to you as the world gives. Do not let your hearts be troubled and do not be afraid.

26. Shalom

Shalom is the name of the most High God!
Shalom is the completeness of form;
Shalom is the welfare of the hurting;
Shalom is the prosperity of the discerning;
Shalom is the soundness of mind!
Shalom is the absence of discord and fight;
Shalom is the state of well-being;
Shalom is the governance of good health;
Shalom is the harmony of the soul!
Shalom is protection from all harm;
Shalom is the expression of calmness;
Shalom is the feeling of contentment;
Shalom is fruitfulness and perfection!
Shalom is the inner and outer peace;
Shalom is the fullness of joy;
Shalom is the true blessing;
Sir Shalom, the promised Messiah,
The soon and coming King,
Is none other than the Prince of peace,
Our Glorious One,
Our Lord and Savior Jesus Christ,
Shalom is the fulfillment of God's purpose!
Shalom …!

Living Word of God
Sharper than any double~edged sword

Isaiah 53:5

But he was pierced for our transgressions,
he was crushed for our iniquities;
the punishment that brought us peace was on him,
and by his wounds we are healed.

27. Son Of Man

Pierced and crushed,
Beaten and whipped,
Man of sorrows,
Carrying our sins.

Drenched in blood,
Crowned with thorns,
Rejected He walked,
True love He taught.

Oppressed and condemned,
Struck down and ashamed,
Unjustly pained,
Without sin got stained.

Bearing the insult,
Not worrying the result,
Sharing the humanness,
His love was like madness.

Sorrow and grief
Befriended Him,
Pain and suffering
Were close to Him.

I Touched The Hem Of His Garment

Restoring the souls,
Rebuilding the walls,
Healing the wounded,
His love never ended.

Living Word of God
Sharper than any double~edged sword

Genesis 9:16

…Whenever the rainbow appears in the clouds, I will see it and remember the everlasting covenant between God and all living creatures of every kind on the earth.

28. Sound Of Rain

When the clouds get dark
And the rain's about to fall;
I close my eyes
And seek Your face,
For something new
You are about to do!

I get excited each time
With the sound of the rain,
For after the rain
The rainbow will show up,
Which is Your promise
Of love I know!

It gives me the hope
To keep going with the flow;
Tells me to trust
The One I owe,
My life my breath
And every single thing
I couldn't let go!

Living Word of God
Sharper than any double-edged sword

1 Peter 5:10

And the God of all grace, who called you to his eternal glory in Christ, after you have suffered a little while, will himself restore you and make you strong, firm and steadfast.

29. Take My Heart Lord, And Hide It Inside Yours

This tender heart of mine,
Though so broken yet is Thine!

You alone can make it whole
O Spirit, take control.

Hope that perished, will be restored
As I hold on to the Sword.

For Thou cherish, to help me endure
Through the process as I mature.

I've been broken, I've been bruised,
By Thy power, I'll sail and cruise.

When the pain grows, the Spirit faints,
All my tears, on Thy heart I will paint.

As I open up my heart for You to see all my grief,
O my Savior, never alone, Thy touch may leave.

Living Word of God
Sharper than any double~edged sword

Matthew 26:28

"This is my blood of the covenant, which is poured out for many for the forgiveness of sins."

Hebrews 9:12

"He did not enter by means of the blood of goats and calves; but he entered the Most Holy Place once for all by his own blood, thus obtaining eternal redemption."

Exodus 12:13

"...The blood will be a sign for you on the houses where you are, and when I see the blood, I will pass over you. No destructive plague will touch you ..."

30. The Blood

The Blood, The Blood, it was The Blood!
The Blood so pure my Savior bled.
Drops of blood, bled all the way,
While carrying the cross on that day.
The Holy Blood, The Worthy Blood,
The Sinless Blood, t'was My Savior's Precious Blood.

The veins that shed The Matchless Blood,
Dried forever, that once carried His Blood!
His side was pierced with a spear,
Gushing the flow of blood and water.
Though we are clay and He is the Potter,
T'was all for the sake of His son and daughter.

The nails that pierced my Savior's hands,
Hands, that once washed the disciples feet,
Now carried His weight upon that cross.
Also the feet, the Holy feet,
That walked for miles for their needs to meet.
Hung upon that wooden cross.

Covered in blood & stained with sin,
Pierced in pain & nailed with shame,
No other death was the same,
But for that very moment He came.
When God to us His gift He sent,
He thought of a way for us to repent.

I Touched The Hem Of His Garment

Thirsty throat, unquenched He went,
Under our sins, He got bent.
Breathed His last, gave up His life,
Put in a rich man's grave.
Third day came and He rose again,
All for my gain, He took away my pain.

The Blood, The Blood, it was The Blood!
The Blood so pure my Savior bled.
Drops of blood, bled all the way,
While carrying the cross on that day.
The Holy Blood, The Worthy Blood,
The Sinless Blood, t'was My Savior's Precious Blood.

(Written in the midst of the world pandemic of 2020)

LIVING WORD OF GOD
SHARPER THAN ANY DOUBLE~EDGED SWORD

Revelation 5:13

Then I heard every creature in heaven and on earth and under the earth and on the sea, and all that is in them, saying:

"To Him who sits on the throne and to the Lamb be praise and honor and glory and power, for ever and ever!"

31. The Lamb Slain For Me, The Lion Who Paid For Me

O Sacred One, O Holy One,
O Resurrected One, O Risen One!

O Precious One, O Loved One,
O Chosen One, O Glorious One!

O King of kings, O Lamb of God,
O Anointed One, O Son of God!

O Exalted One, O Majestic One,
O Ruling Monarch, O God Who Reigns!

O Healer God, O Great Physician,
O Righteous One, O Deliverer!

O Giving God, O Provision Maker,
O Living Bread, O Generous One!

O God of lightening, O God of thunder,
O God of the storms, O God of calm seas!

O God of strength, O God of might,
O God of fire, O God of victory!

O God of love, O God of wisdom,
O God the Father, Spirit and Son!

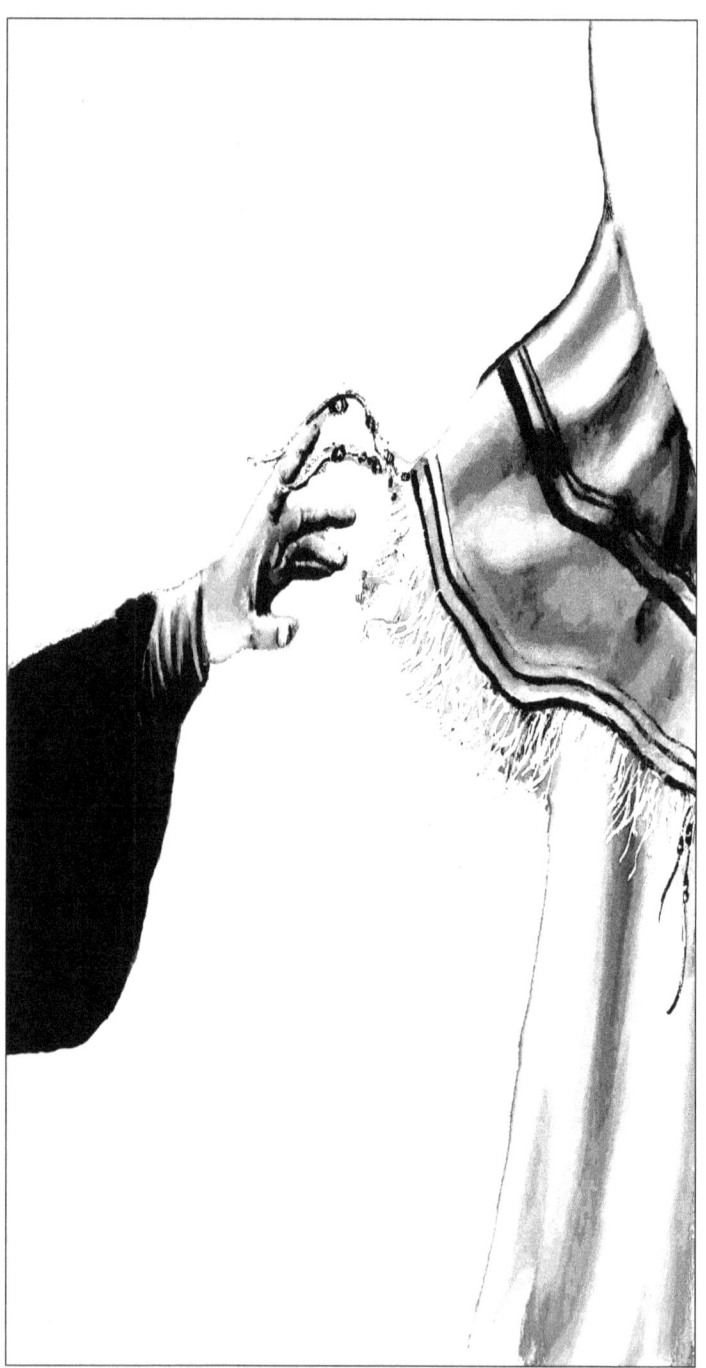

My all in all, my everything,
The Lord of heavens and the earth!

I sing for you, I cry for you,
I clap for you, I bow down to you!

You are the Lamb, slain for me,
Yet the Lion, Who paid for me.

LIVING WORD OF GOD
SHARPER THAN ANY DOUBLE~EDGED SWORD

Matthew 6:10

… Your kingdom come,
your will be done,
on earth as it is in heaven …

Matthew 5:13-16

… You are the salt of the earth …

You are the light of the world … In the same way, let your light shine before others, that they may see your good deeds and glorify your Father in heaven.

32. The Light And The Salt

Yes Lord, not mine, but Thy will be done.
Till Your will becomes my will,
Till Your heart becomes my heart,
Till Your desire becomes my one true desire,
I pray, O Lord, not mine, but Thy will be done.

For the rest of my life,
You walk by my side,
For You are my sweetest guide,
I will leave my pride,
And be Your humble bride.

Catch me O Lord, each time I fall,
Help me dear God, so I can stand tall,
Praising Thy name, to You I will call,
The King of heaven, I will exalt,
By being the light and the salt.

You have washed me, made me clean,
You have created, my innermost being,
You have planned my life to be green,
You are my Savior, on You I will lean,
Through my life, may You be seen.

Living Word of God
Sharper than any double-edged sword

Matthew 28:1-10

After the Sabbath, at dawn on the first day of the week, Mary Magdalene and the other Mary went to look at the tomb. There was a violent earthquake, for an angel of the Lord came down from heaven and, going to the tomb, rolled back the stone and sat on it. His appearance was like lightning, and his clothes were white as snow. The guards were so afraid of him that they shook and became like dead men. The angel said to the women, "Do not be afraid, for I know that you are looking for Jesus, who was crucified. He is not here; he has risen, just as he said. Come and see the place where he lay. Then go quickly and tell his disciples: 'He has risen from the dead and is going ahead of you into Galilee. There you will see him.' Now I have told you." So the women hurried away from the tomb, afraid yet filled with joy, and ran to tell his disciples. Suddenly Jesus met them. "Greetings," he said. They came to him, clasped his feet and worshiped him. Then Jesus said to them, "Do not be afraid. Go and tell my brothers to go to Galilee; there they will see me."

33. The Resurrection ~ Afraid Yet Filled With Joy

It was the Sunday morning,
The new day was dawning,
The women had been sobbing,
And the earth started quaking.

The heavens were opening,
The Lord's angel descending,
His face shone like lightning,
White as snow was his clothing.

The tomb stone started rolling,
And on it the angel was sitting,
The guards in fear trembling,
Fell to the ground fainting.

Those women came looking,
Early morning they had quickened,
When to Him they were crucifying,
From a distance they were watching.

Finding His body no longer there lying,
Looking at the other, without even saying,
He isn't here! From the dead He is risen!
Just as He said, their eyes had seen the vision.

To spread the news they went rushing,
To the disciples who were crushing,
Afraid yet filled with joy, worshiping
The King who is coming!

Living Word of God
Sharper than any double~edged sword

Matthew 11:28

Come to me, all you who are weary and burdened, and I will give you rest ...

1 Peter 5:7

Cast all your anxiety on him because he cares for you.

34. Time And Time Again

Time and time again,
Man has failed me, Lord!

Time and time again,
Man has proved his worth.

The more I trust in You,
The less I lean on man.

The more I have of You,
The less of fear I have.

The more I abide in You,
The less of worry I feel.

The strong I grow in You,
Your love and power I feel.

The more I get from You,
The more I give the world.

I lay down all to You,
Pour it down at Your feet.

Would You accept, O Lord,
This offering of a humble heart?

All praise belongs to You,
For You deserve it all!

LIVING WORD OF GOD
SHARPER THAN ANY DOUBLE~EDGED SWORD

Psalm 84:2

*My soul yearns, even faints,
for the courts of the LORD;
my heart and my flesh cry out
for the living God.*

John 4:14

… but whoever drinks the water I give them will never thirst. Indeed, the water I give them will become in them a spring of water welling up to eternal life.

35. Water My Soul

Come Lord and come Lord and water my soul,
Dry and thirsty, I stand at Your door.
Mercy & compassion flows from Your throne,
Holding Your Word, to You I will call.

Love that is endless and love that is true,
Fills me with power, and fills me with hope,
Tells me to trust in the Father above,
Pour out Your oil, and I'll be whole.

Where there is darkness, Your light will shine,
Led by the cloud, You promised to guide,
When I am failing, my strength You will be,
When I was wailing, Your hand set me free.

Way that is narrow, that will I choose.
Bringing You honor, nothing to loose,
Life that is worthy, and life that is clean,
Walking with You, on pastures green!

Living Word of God
Sharper than any double~edged sword

Matthew 16:15-16

"But what about you?" he asked. "Who do you say I am?"

Simon Peter answered, "You are the Messiah, the Son of the living God."

36. Who Do You Say I Am?

I say, You are:
The Mighty Healer
The Wise Teacher
The Anointed Preacher
The Promise Keeper
The Skillful Creator
The Integrous Leader
The Chain Breaker
The Peacemaker
The Lost-Seeker
The Faithful Provider
The Relationship Builder
The Determined Lover
The Life Giver
The Holy Ruler
The serpent-Crusher
The Problem Solver
The Gentle Shepherd
The Humble Servant
The Prayer Warrior
The Master Planner
The Match Maker
The Soul Winner
The Abundant Restorer
The Suffering Endurer
The Miracle Worker
The Way Maker

The Generous Forgiver
The Hope Giver
The Loving Father
The Wonderful Counselor
The King Eternal
The Risen Savior
You are Christ the Messiah, the Son of the living God!
That's who You are.

LIVING WORD OF GOD
SHARPER THAN ANY DOUBLE~EDGED SWORD

GENESIS 1:3~4

And God said, "Let there be light," and there was light. God saw that the light was good, and he separated the light from the darkness.

JOHN 8:12

When Jesus spoke again to the people, he said, "I am the light of the world. Whoever follows me will never walk in darkness, but will have the light of life."

37. Yeshua ~ The Light Of The World

When darkness covered the face of the earth,
The Spirit of God lit the way!
King of the universe, Light of the world
Sent us a hopeful ray!

Lamp stand of God illuminated the world,
His glory filled the heavens and the earth,
He never dwelt in a temple made with hands,
His majesty and splendor is way too grand!

Centre light, set ablaze by the Father of lights,
Burns the hearts with passion & fire
Of those who are seeking The Kings return,
And waiting upon His Holy Fire!

In Him there is no darkness,
He promises the light of life.
He is the revealer of mysteries,
He knows what lies in secrets!

When people were drowning in their sin,
And innocent lives were going astray,
The Light of the world showed up,
So His people won't ever sway!

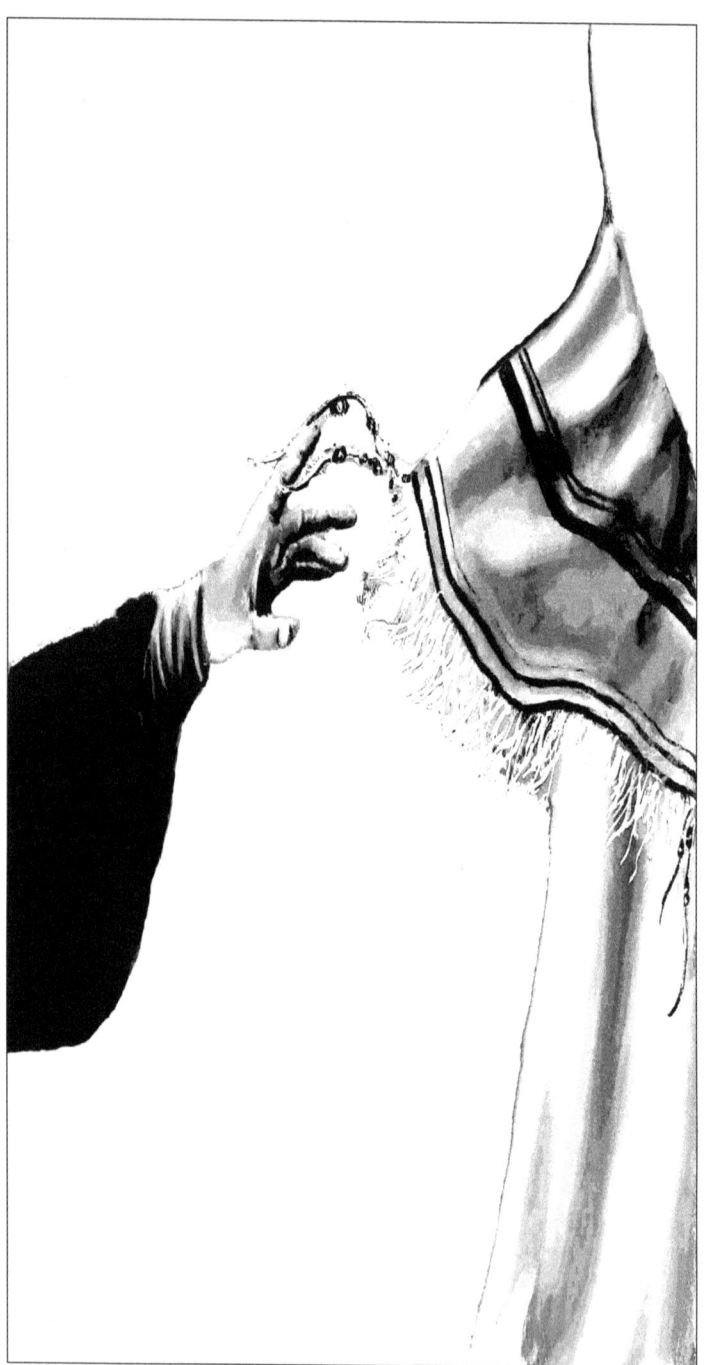

His life brought light to one and all,
The light of His Word gave life to us all,
In the darkness, as He would shine,
Opened the eyes that were blind!

His image bearer on earth,
Now I am.
The flame of fire
And the salt and light I am!

I Touched The Hem Of His Garment And Healing He Gave To Me ...

Shalom the fulfillment of God's promise was born on September 8th, 2017. We all waited expectantly for this moment to arrive when we would take our little princess home and our loving family of four would turn to five. But God tweaked His plans a bit and we had to wait at the hospital for exactly 115 days before we could finally reunite as a family.

As the nurse presented Shalom to her dad, when she opened her beautiful mouth with a loud cry, what he saw was that the roof of her mouth had an opening that was not familiar. Her chin looked small and no one knew her tongue was a little tiny too. Her little jaw was sitting further back than normal and she was diagnosed with Pierre Robin Sequence and had a cleft palate. Shalom came into the world struggling to breathe.

Considering the complications, Shalom was transported to one of the largest children's hospital in Fort Worth, Texas. She was handed over to the best team of doctors and was seen by various specialists and went through multiple procedures. Doctors discovered that Shalom was born with two holes in her heart which eventually got filled on its own.

After almost two months at the hospital, one fine Friday we had a decision-making meeting. We were advised by the doctors and surgeons about a surgical intervention for Shalom. The procedure was called the jaw distractors, and involved enlarging her jaw in the hope that it would help with her breathing. Her breathing was so unsafe that doctors even talked about sending Shalom back home only on a breathing monitor and with a special car seat, specifically designed for babies with breathing issues. We became deeply troubled and had no peace about the surgery. We called out to God to save our daughter and pleaded to bypass the jaw surgery, as that surgery sounded quite invasive and involved breaking her jaw. I reminded God of the scripture where none of Jesus' bones were broken in John 19:36 and hence to protect Shalom's jawbone too.

The incident that followed the next Monday was that Shalom developed a viral flu (a blessing in disguise). This common cold infection prohibited the surgeon from touching Shalom for any surgery till she was four weeks virus free. It was such a relief for us as it gave us time to fasten ourselves in prayer and to seek God's face and His healing touch upon Shalom in a miraculous way. We claimed the scripture where the touch of Jesus' hand would heal everyone (Luke 4:40).

The miraculous intervention happened when God Himself gave growth to Shalom's chin and after two months of laying alternatively either on her right or left side, Shalom could easily lie on her back without dropping her oxygen level. Her tongue grew a little and didn't fall back anymore. The surgeon came back saying, she doesn't need the jaw distractors as her breathing has improved on its own. We rejoiced in our hearts seeing the touch of the Master. The Healing God, the Miracle-Worker, was constantly interceding and mediating on behalf of Shalom.

God was not just looking after Shalom, He supernaturally provided an army of prayer warriors from various groups and churches to pray for Shalom's healing. Various friends and Pastors visited us at the hospital with the words of hope and encouragement, making our journey easier. 24 hour prayer chains were held for Shalom and even different prayer lines continually made intercession, requesting God for Shalom's healing. Our home Church strongly stood by us, when we were going through this massive ordeal at the hospital. Even though we were going through this traumatic experience, we knew that God was carrying us in His very own hands. He was speaking very clearly through His Word and was guiding us continually.

Almost four months at the hospital seemed like forever but I felt peace in my heart when I surrendered Shalom to the Lord and went about praying for other NICU mothers at the hospital. That made my journey a lot easier as I shifted my focus from my own problems and it gave me a mission, to share the love of God with the broken hearted.

As for Shalom, her battle was not over yet. The feeding was still an issue. She could not go home till she ate safely. Shalom was not fed orally for over 6 months of her life because of the possibility of aspiration, which could cause the milk to get into her lungs and then could develop into pneumonia or another problem. Later after a long wait, she was operated on for a gastrostomy tube. We were constantly living under a threat about her breathing, feeding, aspiration, etc.

Then the day came when it seemed like our chains were broken. Nothing had changed in the natural, but we knew it in the Spirit, the season had shifted for us, for good. Shalom was discharged from the hospital on December 31st on a cold, snowy day.

God's timing was strategic and on the New Year's morning, Shalom opened her eyes in her own home in the presence of her most loving family. God proved His faithfulness to us. After two months of being home, with excessive trials and lot of prayers, Shalom started eating and drinking by mouth and never developed any of the chest infections or ear infections that were possible, and the gastrostomy tube was also taken out. She has been doing everything so beautifully. God amazed us with His goodness.

Our God is a God of miracles. We believe that because Jesus lives, so shall Shalom live an amazing and abundant life.

In May 2020, Shalom got operated for her cleft palate repair. With much prayer covering, Shalom went for surgery. Many saints prayed for Shalom's complete healing and a successful surgery was performed. God had her covered beautifully. We believe the God who created the heavens and the earth by His great and mighty power and infinite wisdom is the same God who has given such profound wisdom and knowledge to the most amazing surgeon Dr. Eric Hubli to do such artistic work with so much skill and expertise. God not only looked after us but also provided us with the best hands to perform Shalom's surgery. We thank and appreciate Dr Hubli very much. We give all glory to our great God.

The Bible says,

Jeremiah 29:11

"For I know the plans I have for you," declares the Lord, "plans to prosper you and not to harm you, plans to give you hope and a future.

Matthew 14:36

As I touched the hem of His garment, healing He gave to me.

Sharing My Heart ...

When I got to know about Shalom's condition, obviously I was very, very angry. I felt betrayed by God. I cried out for days, "it's not fair, God!" I asked Him, "The creator of the heavens and the earth, the One who was watching over Shalom's unformed body and the One who was having great thoughts and good plans about Shalom - how could He miss out on such important detail of her life? What made Him, pick Shalom and us for this battle, especially when we love Him so much?"

I asked Him, "where did we go wrong, God?" "What happened that you had to allow this?" "What made you angry at us?" I said, "God, I don't wish this upon anyone, and I am not as good as you are, so you being such a loving Father, how could you allow this to happen to us, who are your very own people, whom you love so much?" "Did it not pain your heart, God?" "What were you thinking?" "You asked me to name her Shalom, which means wholeness, then why is there a hole in her mouth? It doesn't make sense to me!" "Were you being ironic?" "Why is her tongue so small?" "You know God, I will go and pray for people anyway!" "You didn't have to get me to this place to get my attention." "You know me God ..." and I would weep and plead with Him, without making a noise ....

Then I started doing what I knew best ... WORSHIPPING HIM. I said, "God, whether all this happened or not," "you know, that all I know, and have always done, is worship you, so I am just going to worship you and thank You, for you alone know what's best." All I ask is this: "use it all for your glory." "I still love you God and I believe if you want to, you can come into this room right now and touch Shalom and give growth to her

tongue" and I started feeling hopeful that God deliberately allowed this, so He could miraculously heal Shalom and give us a visitation.

I kept waiting in the hospital room every night for Jesus to come and visit us. I started to think, this could be our moment to meet Jesus. I told Shalom repeatedly that, "no one but Jesus can come and heal you. He is our only hope." I started to worship and pray with her. I would make her sit on my lap and read the Bible to her. If I had to leave the room to go and eat, I would leave the worship music playing for Shalom and I would pray to Jesus to give charge to His healing angels all around Shalom's bedside.

In spite of all the questions, God was purifying us. It seemed like going through a fiery process.

Things I learned from my journey ...
- As I magnified God in the storm, the storm became so small in front of His mighty power.
- Jesus never ever brought any sickness upon anyone. All He brought was healing and He still does. Jesus is the only healer.
- As many as touched Him, His touch made them all well and they received their healing (Matthew 14:36).
- Only God can make things grow (1 Corinthians 3:7).
- Miracles happen today since Jesus Christ is the same yesterday, and today and forever (Hebrews 13:8).
- Seek the Kingdom of God above all else, and live righteously, and He will give you everything you need (Matthew 6:33).
- Those who sow with tears will reap with songs of joy (Psalm 126:5).
- Jesus said, "Did I not tell you that if you believe, you will see the glory of God" (John 11:40)?

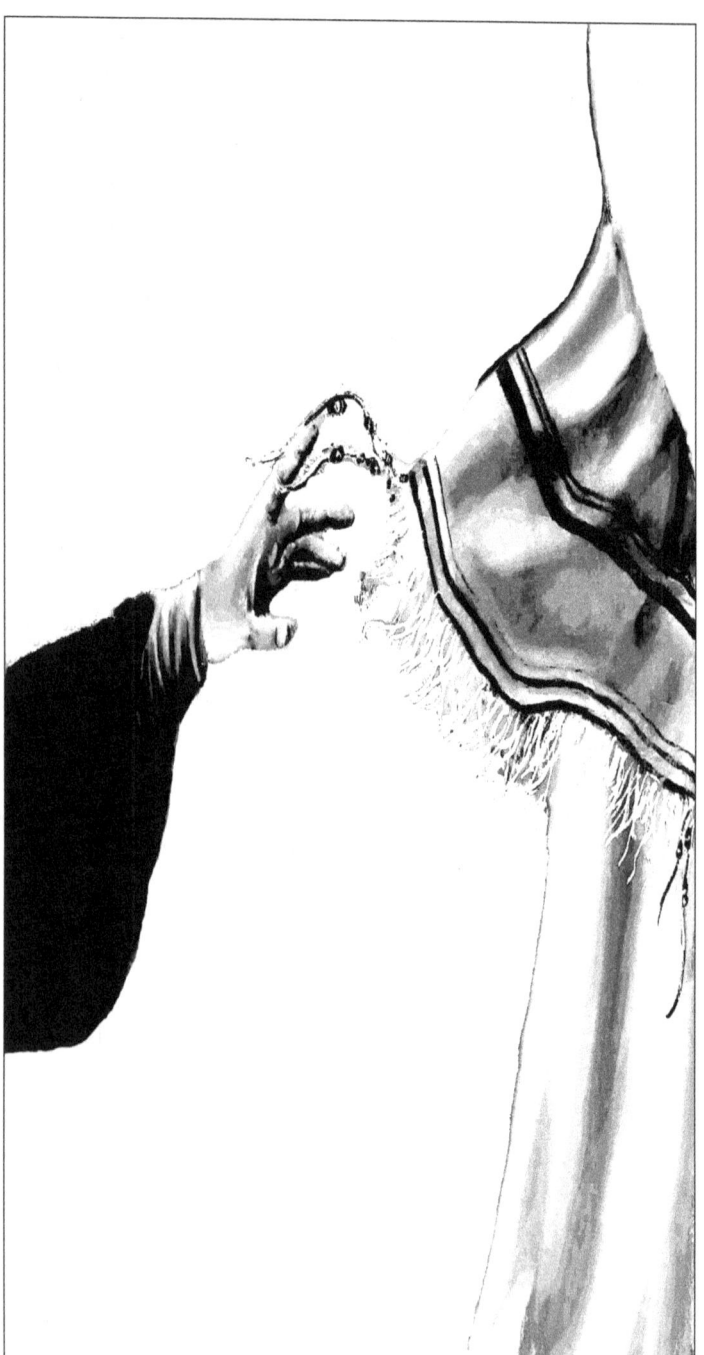

About The Author

Vandana (Vini) Pandya is a homemaker of an incredibly amazing man of God Tejas, her God sent life-partner. They have three beautiful children. Vini loves expressing her heart out in the form of poetry. She is an author, a speaker, a counselor and a worshipper. She considers her greatest strength is to have been blessed with a heart of worship and service.

Vini originates from a Hindu family who has been transformed by the light of Christ. She has found immense joy and treasure in knowing the God whom she can worship in Spirit and in Truth. She believes it is by shear grace that she has been saved and doesn't want to see people perishing in ignorance because no one shared with them, the Truth that she has found.

Vini's deep desire is to see people knowing their identity in Christ. By the power of the Holy Spirit, she excellently counsels and encourages the fallen and the lost.

She considers that prayer, prayer and deep prayer has been the reason and the driving force of her ministry.

She encourages the readers to come alongside and enjoy the pearl of great price, the hidden treasure of the Bible, the darling of heaven and the soon and coming King Jesus Christ!

www.ingramcontent.com/pod-product-compliance
Lightning Source LLC
LaVergne TN
LVHW051500070426
835507LV00022B/2859